RANK

KUHL HOUSE POETS

edited by Mark Levine and Emily Wilson

RANK

Poems by Aaron McCollough

University of Iowa Press, Iowa City

University of Iowa Press, Iowa City 52242

www.uiowapress.org
Printed in the United States of America

Design by Ashley Muehlbauer

The University of Iowa Press is a member of Green Press Initiative and is committed to preserving natural resources.

Printed on acid-free paper

Library of Congress Cataloging-in-Publication Data
McCollough, Aaron.
Rank : poems / by Aaron McCollough.
pages cm. — (Kuhl House poets)
ISBN 978-1-60938-389-3 (pbk),
ISBN 978-1-60938-390-9 (ebk)
I. Title.
PS3613.C37A6 2015
811'.6—dc23 2015008710

This book is dedicated to Suzanne

Alack, 'tis he! Why, he was met even now
As mad as the vex'd sea, singing aloud,
Crown'd with rank fumiter and furrow weeds,
With harlocks, hemlock, nettles, cuckoo flow'rs,
Darnel, and all the idle weeds that grow
In our sustaining corn.

—SHAKESPEARE

RANK

I CAN embrace life
chestnut tangles outside
and inside two coffee cups
on our glass table
embrace

yet in these meditations
often desire
the retaining wall's shadow
clockwise in one burial
warren, shielding each other,
retaining the shadow's
long frame leaning out

history owns this much
framed papyri lined up like little counties
the remnant less than nothing
my fabrics and yours, touching

I GUESS an iceflow came through
to take the road.
I can only guess that would
destroy these remains slowly,
grass leaves twig thread drain
in the cauldron sewer called foothill,
in the foothill. Attendance,
a pledge is empty; not
your creature,
however tight the passage. No
the land is sifting off slow
with withered plants and silk, good rank
seeping always down and on,
ungraspable, plying stronger
agent to believe in, revise
my faith in unbelief, weak,
rank, ancient, I guess and guess
even pinched I would, with wind
in grass, not belong to any moment
nor believe in.

Only units with no faith, no interest,
poetry.

More rushing between the cracks,
winter cracking the foundation.
The old stump coming apart
in big chunks and round katabasis;

a spiral stairwell shimmies
under any weight,
absolute as sand.

A tree falls in the world's witness,
fungal sum and cephalanthous
triumphs in hearing, we depend
with the spider in the window,
the sun's endless tunnel, our shell,
a haze on the frontier,

outline of the flame and all
its inner varieties.

Feather and split. The woods sing out
to welcome the coming judgment,
a wood may go on forever.
What's blue's title? I'm alive as fuse.
What's lit by ash and unlit?
All invisible eccentricities
in an arrow in the snow,
spring's terrible words, paths,
lightning hideaways, inflamed ways in
and sticks scattered rather than bound.

A closed fist galaxy.
The center of a wagon wheel, a hole.
I live here.

The limits still sluice moss.
A ticking complaint rises
to the only noise in the yard.
Stand in the noise, your radial arms
pulled lazy with the moment's
octopodal weight, with the sea's
receding influence.
Noise is metaphysical.
By whatever induction we mark it,
this one note indicates a din.

Lichen covered slivers of limestone
bowing in the middle with some full gaps:
the world is coming,

not the world, what's coming is
earth, clay expelling water
after ice expelling clay, over years,

or, a world; one accessed
above another.

THE NAKED bones, especially the head,
a small, fettering memento

a year with two seasons moves
only as quickly as a year

as sure as its moments measure
safe as skin

a certainty unfolds to be certain
and shimmers in the silver rayed guitar
a way to move towards morning
should you seek me, you may find a flower

—

the power not put out chugs on in the dark
as light breaking on a slope shelf
schools of minnows angle away from us
anemone. daughter of wind, wind flower

—

I could kill for the songs, I could,
common little self, winking rain
clapping with the crowd alone in my room
as concentration pools in the flower

With proper care this may last
where the round guitar begins
against the fourth wall, a wheeling gray
with pixeled edges artificial flower

—

Where the river makes a delta
shear shining and never the same
top of the fairground, the antenna top
twice as close as the flower

—

Sinister can be better, sister.
The urchin glacier conflict
land of abundant roses, soldiers
in the snow. Each flower encased in glass

Owing to a sacred infrastructure,
bone meat skin
wave ambidextrous other matters
out of gaps in shale shine fossil flowers

—

Someone's coughing in another room,
getting over it. Wall clouds guitar.
Wall clouds voices. Being in a body
in an apartment, not being in a flower

—

Flower being and apartment being
Feedback coming from the guitar
lying on the bed and my pulse coiling
in the soil in the bed outside

do you wonder what traps an esteemed man
a fountain wreath painted from a guitar
egg-shell-chipped shining from summer dew
this tessellation of knit flowers

—

to smear some giant crumb over the skin
"whatever light there is"
sunburst to soften paving tar
on which moss grows but no flower

—

a permanent (as earth, as shell, as skin)
record sustains the silent guitar
and its rushed out waves, rushing
on the sloping shelves galaxy

SEIZED THERE where the thesis is
clouded and clotted in the junipers
halfway down a tall slow wave
under too much responsibility.
One branch screwed on another
with roots punching from the stone wall
one long seam from the bright insides
must be bending.

Placed on a hill in a cuddle of bones
knit with soft effects between two seas
sodden hair clot here, swath of bark
wheeling beneath the trail.
I couldn't catch breath
(knit with tender appointments)
and stood to lose my place.

Respecting natural boundaries
lake lapped coasts of the ice peninsula
respectfully declining.
The kingdom was never more
than some inflated local
piece of the movement.

I caught breath.
Saw the strings before I heard them.
The bars, the topographic rings.

Lord of this puddle,
treat it well. Well-meaning harm,
your measure and rule.

CAN'T FEEL the sun

one face after
the certainty in the gate latching
with its sympathy or another face
in far enough properties behind
sore scores, a storm settled, wound up
to a gelid chime

great heaviness by the wall, the sneer
breaching underneath, escapes
in a keystone, stroke turning
on its shadow

the largest outposts
on the head of, the stroke of strict green

soft but sharp, if slow, if legible
alone as a sting at depth
urge hardening toward a season
pushes out passages to a front

hot with the insult
until a birthmark sets, settles, cracks
in the green dry wind
not unafraid

I LOOK into the black bird's black planet
for lake, some sustenance, for ice
a smokestack view with green conundrum
dredge in the black eye flower

—

A silhouetted tree of the morning
disordered sense desired damask
has languor never language, formed
in shadow against light in full shower

—

songbird-construed clouds resembling flowers

the hour upon us again
as small hands chime
pattern a hoof, helmet, papyrus
shred anything we know

—

Outside the capsule of the self but not
so far you're alone, guitar
Listen
to the fugue, a word for flower

—

My own dull animal shell
my own dull cell
strings slept together and woke
as Spring asserts

It keeps inside a box it makes a home
inside a case inside a mouth
They stay behind, belonging
where nothing rises

—

Inside the cloak is OK with withering
anticipated, dry guitar intoned
still numbers, and crumbling down
(the cloak included) goes the sunflower

—

Headlights swept the extremities sharply
self-semblance struck the string of the guitar
in puff & hum,
louder than roots

WAKING ESCAPES from a hole somewhere;
eye of one season beside another,
winter and spring of the same old face
turning, not unsurprised, at sun's hail
in the longer morning of this place
and the longer dusk, slow announcing
purlieus, cold sun horn in water.

In a sling as regards time, blindfold
in muslin, utterly swaddled,
cocooned not at a beginning, not
at an ending but in a middle
and a middle again
                    the damaged bird's sidewalk yawning

I open and close upon the day
and open and close
a sharp tree among the blurry ones
blue fir between blue pines

in my party are the bodies and places,
the feelings and movements,
the words for a total but more
than words or total   in my rank,
unpruned,
unpruned

glare in my eyes,
some warmth still in the window,

the fan silent, a snow just begun
uniform

sleep is not the picture of death here
though one way to handle such pictures

NOT FLAWS. Signatures.
Impression in cellulose darker, lighter
a third season forgotten.

All the tassel tips grass, all shiver.
Cold hollow down this little
steeple, murky gathering more foam,
a secular brook detaches and
another so on, sound
along all the lines, spilled all the bends
until still or somewhere under hill.

Nothing inanimate that may be touched.

Nothing unremarked.

"The tree of life or trees," "rigor," "mercy."

You must accept your disappearance
by learning to disappear politely,
the shadow lean from great light
and frivolous impediment.

Still. Under hill.
Tree. Separation.
Long grasses in accord.

Long and short flaws — not flaws — circumstance,
deciduous scrabbles —

Something less
also lessoned, a new difficulty.

IN THIS many analogued book of animals
a twitching branch is right,
framed in skies added past measure
adduced with feeling's waves on the skin
as a two-step and rigid fluid
with the perfect pitch of the chorale
discernable to each, as a switch,
down to each voice, each minor death—
adolescent squirrel washed from a hole,
eyes bold past the manifold, just off,
out of colloidal unseen gutters.

That each station of my movement swells
with humus and repels it—
were a stump eroding in a shining bath,
were the high-heavens decay unsmelt—
is merely accurate, but as they are
thus, the swelling splits the abutment,
the thrum grows acute,
the glass breaks, leaks, and stains a shirt.
Sound in the service of music,
unwound but recoiling, the worm, the weed,
all raw bodies in the thicket,
densest in the middle, the present bog.
Even in the middlest mire,
a single and certain saving sin.

A heaven if not also another place,
a filthy nest, runs along on wheels,
gangs of legs, or pressed by the low wind.

That is a camera which must feed
but never rest and vegetal film,
a kingdom in case, in cases.
A sound, an image, a blow.
A sundered tether, tied intestinally
in knots that should not fit the given.

the buried wire erupts with the vine
and the strings choke the juniper
wind in the guitar, an acrid home signal
floating above the bulb

—

water in the pine bark and spoiled firmness
everywhere at plank ends swamp foam
radiating with the rains
ankle deep

—

entirely deep as to swallow whole
little movements
complaining or waving with the gesture
sweeping strings

I can see you in mud,
concocted, connected to
lines charged fungal in a mopey array
called the vault

—

all the animal songs by the river garden
hundred claw fingers single strings
stubbling progress to be mown by a
corner of the park invasive flowers

—

suburban remove, by a rain garden
sirens, diesel, exhaust, guitar
invasive, conclusive, mosquito
what? what flower?

call them movements, touches, even feels
call them vignettes for upright guitar,
a temple layered with only the sounds
material or petals

—

flower says the birds leaves path bench flower
invading each other as guitar
in tiny hairs of the canal
and the foot in the grass shaped flower

—

crow softens the bone in the puddle,
lumbers up a dark slide
and won't crow this way for fear of losing
marl for marrow for a high nest

NOT UNDONE by length—declining
by terrace. Earth and light
at the manifold and great grass downstairs
stages of shadow in a day, an instance,
impossible tax,
heat and moisture on skin or fur,
one fume in the mundane censer,
smooth as you please, water through teeth.

Day arises, or it grows
little threads in dark ground,
lugged beneath a vine
polluted in a parterre
but still living, reaching hands uneven,
near numb,
terrible noise
in the hole at its base.

This existence and its noise.
Our noise in a tall slow wave
in the thalweg,
a curve squared in the moment
with a minor signature,
now sour
on the table in the dim room.

SLOW HERE, take a seat here.

We expand

opening oak. Swelling, sweating,

coming dank rings.

Tunnel with a light, only light,

horse color valley

and sweetness.

Escape, fond animals,

livid horizon.

Soon it will be done, it may be fine.

It came from the left

blinking huskily suffering senescent,

a campfire against some old bricks

and someone spit

copper over the back of a hand,

in reverse.

We retreating objects give thanks for every moment.

In the city, the tar   in the country, manure

one star and precocious life,

an immunity.

By fear and ease and nothing between,

we may find these waves, curved points,

bubbles, foam.

Little dog. Little acarina upon.

Otherwise, so much self. Sky.

SLICE OF fruit and cigarette slice of
flower on his way to the underworld
who wanted to touch mist.

Sis, the skin is not opaque so
the fire in the hearth is a window.
I try to hear you singing.

Grass between the thumbs and holes
in the sky's vellum
but the pieces make sense,

enough sense to begin, so your face
in the window lights this corner of the bed,
and there I lay out the pieces.

Tonight a storm all over the roof,
tomorrow twig and devastation,
how is this not all?

We must not know for sure.
To follow the song far enough, foolishly enough,
backward, we are inclined, because of joy.

Gully ways and speeds, creases in
the organism, which is a hill
or pit.

The corners gnawed,
the joint between shoulder and head extending,
so an ear might be lent, a dint of breeze.

The enormously bolted cinder.
Terrific arch over little screens
we make of our deep brushes with joy.

STAYING IN a little cabin in the city.

Confused by windshield wipers squealing
a metal machine
clapped to a chain link fence in the night,

and stannic croaks

and alarms

electric birds

Over by the Sheraton,
the water is moving fast,
constrained by big and round
or sharp rocks, another element
leaping against itself.

Deep, evening breaths
in these hard, wet sheets
of evening—the chest
will permit these moments room
and also pass them on.
Even forks can be my forks
in part without a wound.

But we are terrified of spring
singing
its metaphors.

ROSE DROOPED, ambulated the neighborhood
in a bee, though drooping balloon;
rose in the light in the heat expanding
as a ruddy bulb

—

Not flying on the wings of warrens,
water lily flight nor falling guitar
over the trails forking along the ridge
then meeting again, feather flowerseed

—

piece out the broken guitar, fan the wood
under the garden with the ground
set shower, set windmill.
Those with ears, those with eyes, let them flower

a dead squirrel threaded tight in the bamboo
bustling with white worms stench static guitar
should you roll in it, no water on earth
should you turn disgusted, no flower

—

lime against the bodies, salt against them
and sand against the bodies and guitar
against the grains sticking
against the moment, pulling to the roots

—

Morning fill up, music peels from the pump
in one flaky layer. Thin guitar.
There is nothing good about this station.
At home, a compensation, no flavor.

I will lie still in bed in the rainstorm,
each line of flight transecting the guitar,
I am of this world not the other,
I think, a wave pulling long warm water.

—

A creature of darkness but only fine
strings wrapping nothing tight,
late summer, no dew left for the flowers.

—

Countless stations, rigging the way here,
home, climbing
ivy, mulch chips falling around green
bundle, cell binder territory.
Another season
seizing the grasshopper.

FROM THE counting house, dread
substantial as throat, substantial as belly,
ambient as bush racket,

breeze against the propeller,
still in the window and a charcoal
distant sign from another house

the bearing of the yard on ridges
trying two sides
so the passage is gray

whatever the need is, grass conducts
hands, arms, trunk's penumbra,
so the need perspires and informs

hiding in the lilac cave
or hustling through the cleanest arcade
a being drawing a heavy sigh

weighs within itself two sacks
of material: the neighborhood in a polished window
and a black ant in water

so goes another division:
two more sprouts
grafted in from outside

and a wandering spirit set out
as emissary
to the nearest reservoir

WALNUT SKULL of some brutal fairy
run afoul of my dog
in the juniper mire
what depends
in these binds,
passion strings,
ivy suckers climbing
the knock kneed craning bridge
to that bright food
can freedom even begin to form
in the morning, reforming blossoms
if we mean to tread with ease
may we move at all

THE SUN really brings out the rot

now distant and close
digested matter digesting the proteins
once allied in digesting the matter

origin / return and a means for considering
the inconsiderable occasion of one's own house

(that which creates and is not created
    that which is neither created nor creates)

but do the fumes rise to his nostrils,
honey-in-mephistis?
is it only time burning on that reeks?

IS SPRING penetrating,
the sanctuary winter laid down
tight, dormered, a crack of light
enough string to wedge in
sleep unswept

waking stem strewn
as many small buds,
and the work suspended,
held in all by one note repeating,
one hand muting the branches

in twin honeyed seasons,
half-measured stemlife
grown wild half inward,
meeting in common, (skirts crisp
with frost wet with dew)
at the end of one long warp

dimpled cells of ice escaping the dark,

aerial roots out on a plain
lull heavy dormers down,
frayed sash cord painted over
the fine green stem

a cell, revealed, a daylight
not a launder, not a gutter,
a passage collapsing on itself
with the twilight

moon flares along river,
sun-film-flecked, the stream ripple:
a day-night-speed light grain
lifting us—bend the distance
strum two habits, world wearing

shine confuses,
speed troubles, matter pools the water

a dam sitting on top
sprouting upside down

mind the sudden knotty stems
frightening little sexes punching up
testing the crust following the string
and rough with juniper hands,
the antic of the enclosure

new unfolding by furlong
to take the whole ground and then return
army's ebb across, a green debris
and growing turn
larger, hungrier, wickeder

the dappled antic hop from many stems
trample on cursive underbrush
for one sentence,
it is all free, to the circle at the boundary
and even beyond

if the kingdom of heaven just stems
from one copse of trees at the riverhead
washing out the frame
tributary rivers feeding soil
laced with rust,
we grow rusty trees
lined with orange dust,
assemble by lacing, lining, stringing
a terrific coat across the lake
to hang from

the person in pictures and mirrors
there being no righteous remnant here
that's only visible to itself
just thin ranks of unrighteousness,
green to brown

a few drops on the thigh
the leg in half a dream broken string
chimes joined at a ring hung on roof nail
withdrawn from basin,
soft tabernacle knit with soft tissue
chassis-work against brute shocks
the desert in full blow

the desert lush but no new stems,
depending nest, swelled junk fistwise
waiting for a surge of predators

in the frame's temple, *faned* icon, stem
to the stable scenes
strung in rings

meridian,
columned up out of the mouth,
still binding from the weight and motion

frost nipping now and sun
now drying out the grass,
lines littering the sky,
embarrassing the page,

beetles grinding in the stem
the shape of the husk of what did live
the stained matter and sound
tumbling along the grain
and makeshift hem

hanged on a stem
our little broken toy, things pass,
a whole day passes, stirring
in the doorframe, staying,
jesting

off the stem. off the stem off the stem
hanged in a domino beneath the moon,
black gloss ant string
to ant jam, ant mound, the precipice
air bead eyes swarming at the septum

it is all living, pruned and curbed,
in frame or out,
all of it is living, empty, grave,

the fiddlehead's palladian stem

RANK THISTLE gone to soft seed
as we know each star sealing
the next change, though change becomes habit
—to work them, not quite luxury grass,
to tramp down, split by the beasts,
to draw new water with the old wine
where the progress is measured with charcoal
in the touching breeze, do us good,
twine the late cool in from the surface
to the slow close canals,
the scent of fennel curling between
warm and cool, the wide white lavender
all cool with a late twinge.

Other crows dawdle more or less patient
while one picks at the carcass
which could be in an attitude of dance
not smashed and split and still,
touching wind to cool touched spot of skin.

Do you fret over a suffering thing
and share your violence

closing a hand around the thistle
for glass cello, suite in e major
pausing in a contrapuntal interim,
stone on stone on stone on stone on stone
on garish gap

whose body, after all, quivering,
mutely opening its beak to God
or a slightly larger beast. now end.

SOMETIMES IN the kingdom of God
in the kingdom of heaven

It is a matter of policy to be free *and* caught
One must turn oneself to do as one ought

and no rest but round contention

MEETING THE welling stream
tremble, rages, raves, it comes,
orchestra, to consult
on matters unfulfilled
whence whisper
all seasons known from a hilltop,

another distemper stunned on the pavement
and rotted newspaper,
pale miscanthus bristles,
soil gone neutral, inches
from an open den, a puckered crux,
thistle in the cold,

and toad, cousin to rock,
slow or still, on its way from a third place

larger than our eyes, our stomachs,
the undigested parts
where the porch remains sound,

or even horizon and toll,

thus familiar,

This trampled down becoming   rant, clear
to the ear of deity,
I mean acorn, green cap, vermin
hollow and ridge of grit,
frozen faucet split to flowstone

with sky in a pool above
or a sink
in a dark cubby, dropped horizontal,
a tonic stretch, little bowl of stars,
or over again on my side
however far sunk within, still here,
beloved, by converging share
lift here again over pendant death,
cradling the neck, spread in scale basket,
asleep in vast moonlight, even,
but spotted together, lasting
organ trails, stones making love,
holding the hill foot
by address and muteness

my all fixed hideout does not gleam
but hovers, a dog nose at the surface

each visit risks
a trip to the flood

Further flexion and knuckle
passed around the morning's crook
is it the last, the first,
fruitful frozen with brown ivy, their droop
—who was just singing, so faint at the hatch,
clogged with long shreds,
crowded with unfinished babies,
in the armed retreat, draped in animals,
a flurry of clucking and song,
the antigen rise in the meter
—a type of soaring
within rigid, invisible lanes

Beyond this brief crest, all, or more again,
   a hinted rest, riot, unpinned

Thin little scores, thin upon themselves,
ribbon running, pointed against their own hearts
or ballooned to theme
: necessities,
shelter, etc. but alone,
one falling, rising, one
long stare in the lodge

each note and pairing now turning for the light
now so barely sensible
sunflower
              sonata pressure

They are leaving   arriving,
neighborhood names on enough tongues
any one tongue can't say it right

sunshine headed to the
village ornament
to the fresh cold return

washing up berries black
ash a fairy tale
with mother buried beneath a tree

worried about
milk flushed faces
visible breath in cabins
the hearse faux proscenium

a chain, a shoe
a millstone
a sifting instrument

good, go tremble, go into the further morning
with its opposite for a beacon

Speaking, or gaping, from a distant hill

at deep dwellings amid a place of stone,

steam ebbs from the stainless face,

breath from glass, the lie, why then,

                                        the creaturely confusion

about the distance between things,

including the wry toes on the bird's foot,

merits our first river

as so much garbage, sheaves of entrails,

as a creature, stepping

after some warmth, too much, too little,

already to satisfy the sterile woods,

love's hewed limit and nature,

a rendition of, at least, eternity

Juniper, erstwhile evergreen,
now rye pale, an arc of light
expands against its vigor, night
and sleep with it, go nowhere

harder than the grade, than the grain
if it carves itself into light thus,
my concern, what I take with me,
a possession inimical

in contest at best with the noises
I build around, but what limit
hasn't moved—that is barely audible,
only plied on across the pile

We're thinking about running
but what mountains and hills to fall under

slowly, night horse, slower please
what would running in the river get us

To catch up with faint, warbling steps
or pass them, careful to land within them
through the near mud, no trace,

or voice in the nobly, worshipfully,
nature-shunned object,

or sit with the technology,
once, almost, elevating,

with the fluorescent abdomen
and lure of last things,

our violent throes, dogs' dreams,

verdigris on the pipe joints,
and the land's warlike phrases

I stepped in anyway, not in malice,
maybe my lower part breaking my fall,
but fault follows a boldness in collapse,
to saturate the ground, to set the soil

for something: a staff rolling on ahead
until it lasts only by assumption   we're leaving
with all our teeth
as the sight appalls us, so we hide

Flying one number for, or bracing to
the basin draining to the sea,
motioned by the winds, a flourishing rash

These little notes stumble, missing part of a foot.
They need our floor only incidentally
slouching with feral cats.

Bless the bat
on its redacted way
to strange
hinges, beyond this quick
blues, walking
together for miles, crying
to exit the image

Best bereft
of something good, and forced
to reckon with
limitation, lank reeds
obscuring us a little,
lifting filth
we made by other moments

on to the sun-speckled curb
which is an abandonment too,
routine, what the bat wobbles over
beneath the satellite
up until now,
your skin,
my nearest alias

Songbirds.
Leaves steeped till sour.
Juniper.
First in the water but no generation.
What do I begin?
A terrific mass, like a star,
invisible, immeasurable,
impossibly remote,
containing every length
and resource.
Time and the remainder.

I am gathering against—myself,
not you, not anyone, but

                                        I'm leaving,
how else to hum with what
is about me
the occasion to endure

ACKNOWLEDGMENTS

Some of the poems in this volume previously appeared in the following places, typically in significantly altered forms: *Colorado Review, Flag+Void, jubilat, Michigan Quarterly Review, Midwestern Gothic, Parallax,* PEN Poetry Series (www.pen.org).

KUHL HOUSE POETS

Christopher Bolin
Ascension Theory

Shane Book
Congotronic

Oni Buchanan
Must a Violence

Michele Glazer
On Tact, & the Made Up World

David Micah Greenberg
Planned Solstice

Jeff Griffin
Lost and

John Isles
Ark

John Isles
Inverse Sky

Aaron McCollough
Rank

Randall Potts
Trickster

Bin Ramke
Airs, Waters, Places

Bin Ramke
Matter

Michelle Robinson
The Life of a Hunter

Robyn Schiff
Revolver

Robyn Schiff
Worth

Rod Smith
Deed

Cole Swensen
The Book of a Hundred Hands

Cole Swensen
Such Rich Hour

Tony Tost
Complex Sleep

Susan Wheeler
Meme

Emily Wilson
The Keep